The Jennifer O'Reilly
Memorial Lecture

IONA

The Jennifer O'Reilly Memorial Lecture Series

The Memorial Lecture in honour of Jennifer O'Reilly was established in 2017 by the School of History, University College Cork. Each year a distinguished scholar is invited to speak on either the age of Bede or medieval iconography, two subjects that Dr O'Reilly explored in her research and teaching.

2017 On Bede and Cassiodorus
Dr Alan Thacker, the Institute of Historical Research.

2018 Venerating the Cross around the year 800 in Anglo-Saxon England
Professor Jane Hawkes, University of York.

2019 At the Ends of the Earth: Conversion and its consequences in some Insular Sources
Professor Máire Herbert, University College Cork.

2020 Insular Art and the Early Medieval Eye: The Codex Amiatinus and the Book of Kells
Dr Carol A. Farr, University of London.

2021 Dynamic Theologies: The Ruthwell Cross from an Irish perspective
Professor Éamonn Ó Carragáin, University College Cork.

2022 Bede and the Spiritual Senses
Professor Arthur Holder, Graduate Theological Union.

2023 *Pater* Ecgberct of Rathmelsigi: The hero of Bede's *Historia Ecclesiastica*?
Professor Dáibhí Ó Cróinín, University of Galway.

Photo: © Dermot Roantree

Dr Jennifer O'Reilly (1943–2016)

Remembered as a gifted lecturer and writer by her colleagues and her students, Dr Jennifer O'Reilly played a key role in establishing the degree programme in History of Art at UCC, where she lectured on medieval history between 1975 and her retirement in 2008. Her scholarly interests and publications lay principally in three areas: the iconography of early Irish and Anglo-Saxon art; the writings of Bede the Venerable and Adomnán of Iona; and medieval hagiography. In these areas she explored the intimate relations between medieval texts and images and the traditions of biblical exegesis shaped by the Church Fathers. Her teaching inspired generations of students, many of whom went on to complete doctorates under her supervision. In retirement she continued to write extensively, and she gave numerous public lectures, including the Jarrow Lecture and the Brixworth Lecture. She was a Member of the Royal Irish Academy and a Fellow of the Society of Antiquaries.

Iona is an imprint of Prosperity Education Limited
Registered offices: 58 Sherlock Close, Cambridge CB3 0HP, United Kingdom

First published 2023

Typesetting and cover design by ORP Cambridge

A catalogue record for this book is available from the British Library

ISBN: 978-1-913825-95-9

The Jennifer O'Reilly Memorial Lecture Series committee:
Terence O'Reilly, Tom O'Reilly, Máirín MacCarron,
Diarmuid Scully, Elizabeth Mullins and Malgorzata D'Aughton

For further information visit:
www.ucc.ie/en/history/drjenniferoreillymemorialpage

The recorded Jennifer O'Reilly Memorial Lectures are available on YouTube.

Printed and Kindle editions of the Jennifer O'Reilly Memorial Lectures are available on Amazon.

The Jennifer O'Reilly
Memorial Lecture
2021

Dynamic Theologies:
The Ruthwell Cross from an Irish perspective

Éamonn Ó Carragáin

A note on the text

This is an updated and expanded version of the online lecture given in April 2021, which is available to watch at: https://youtu.be/jB6NfWSmQRs

The references in this memorial lecture have been limited to four works:

EMTI 1 Jennifer O'Reilly. Carol A. Farr and Elizabeth Mullins, (eds), *Early Medieval Text and Image 1. The Codex Amiatinus, the Book of Kells, and Anglo-Saxon Art.* London: Routledge, 2019.

EMTI 2 Jennifer O'Reilly. Carol A. Farr and Elizabeth Mullins, (eds), *Early Medieval Text and Image 2. The Insular Gospel Books*. London: Routledge, 2019.

HHBE Jennifer O'Reilly. Máirín MacCarron and Diarmuid Scully (eds), *History, Hagiography and Biblical Exegesis.* London: Routledge, 2019.

R&R Éamonn Ó Carragáin, *Ritual and the Rood: Liturgical Images and the Old English Poems of the Dream of the Rood Tradition*. (University of Toronto Press, 2005).

The illustrations have been adapted from W.G. Collingwood, *Northumbrian Crosses of the Pre-Norman Age*. (London: Faber & Gwyer, 1927), with permission from University College Cork:

Fig. 98	p. 26
Fig. 101	p. 15 and p. 39
Fig. 135	p. 5

For further references and a detailed bibliography, colour images and links to chants, see the information provided online at:
https://doi.org/10.5281/zenodo.7683804

Dynamic Theologies: The Ruthwell Cross from an Irish perspective

It was a great honour to be invited to commemorate Jennifer O'Reilly: a first-class scholar, a brilliant teacher, and a most generous and supportive friend. Coming to Ireland, she explored the European monastic culture which Britain and Ireland shared in the early Middle Ages. We shared many years of teaching together: particularly in our joint course on 'Art and Literature in the Middle Ages', which ran for some thirty years (1977–2007).

I began my talk where Jennifer would have liked me to begin: by welcoming Dame Rosemary Cramp, one of the webinar audience that afternoon. Over many years, we at Cork have looked on Rosemary as a beneficent presiding spirit. We are proud to have proposed her in 2006 for an honorary D.Litt. of the National University of Ireland.

1. The Ruthwell Project

I first met Rosemary Cramp when she came to lecture on '*Beowulf* and Archaeology' at UCC in winter 1975. Her lecture admitted that it was difficult to make direct links between *Beowulf* and particular archaeological objects. In her peroration, however, Rosemary pointed to the Ruthwell Cross and its runic poem, where an interdisciplinary approach was essential. After the lecture, I suggested to her that the liturgical innovations of Sergius I (pope 686–701) might be relevant to Ruthwell. Before leaving Cork she invited me to join the team of scholars studying that monument: 'we hadn't thought of liturgy' she remarked. As the only Irish member of the team, I took it as my job to explore how the surviving Irish high crosses might help us to understand Ruthwell: though later, they might provide significant contrasts as well as continuities. The Ruthwell monument is certainly pre-Viking, probably best dated to the mid-third of the eighth century (730–60). By the ninth and tenth centuries, when the major Irish high crosses were erected, the

Viking invasions were well under way. However, a large number of Irish crosses survived that time, and later iconoclasms, more or less undamaged. Irish scholars often do not need to reconstruct iconographic programmes from fragments; they get used to 'reading' each cross as a connected statement. Might this habit embolden us to 'read' Ruthwell too as unified and coherent? The crosses and manuscripts of our two islands shared a common European visual language, though they reflected different 'dialects' of it and they may have come from different centuries. It was good to have as a colleague Jennifer O'Reilly, a subtle interpreter of our common European visual and symbolic heritage.[1]

2. Saints Paul and Anthony

The obvious way for me to start was to examine the panels on Irish crosses depicting the earliest Egyptian monks, Saint Paul the first hermit and Saint Anthony the abbot. The Ruthwell Cross has the earliest surviving Insular depiction of these saints; uniquely it names them and states that they 'broke the loaf [*panem*] in the desert'. In his 'Life of Paul the first hermit', St Jerome had told how the little-known Egyptian hermit Paul was fed in his desert hermitage by a raven who brought him half a loaf each day. When the famous Abbot Anthony found out his desert dwelling, the raven provided a whole loaf for the two of them. Hermit and Abbot now began a courteous argument, each urging the other to have the honour of breaking the loaf. Eventually they agreed to break it together. Many Irish and Pictish examples show the two monks seated to their meal, and almost all depict the bird (raven or, on some crosses, dove, as George Henderson has pointed out) who brought their loaf. But at Ruthwell the saints stand in flowing robes, and there is no bird to distract us: figures and *titulus* alike direct us to the act of breaking in order to share. This panel seems to refer, not directly to Jerome's Life of St Paul, but primarily to a custom implied by an episode in Adomnán's Life of St Columba (I, 44). It would seem that the Iona monks customarily invited priests who came to visit, to break the communal Eucharistic loaf together with the abbot. Perhaps Columba himself, founder as well as abbot, had been inspired by reading

1 For example, EMTI 1, Chapters 4 and 6; EMTI 2, Chapters 4 and 8; HHBE, Chapters 3, 5 and 12.

Jerome to institute such a custom of courteous welcome. However, one day he declined to break the loaf with one Crónán, a visitor from Munster, far off in the south of Ireland. He had been inspired to see that Crónán was a bishop humbly travelling incognito. Columba though a powerful abbot was only a priest: he knew that his visitor, being a bishop, should have the honour of breaking the loaf alone as was done by bishops ('episcopali ritu'). Columba at one stroke both won the contest in courtesy and affirmed the liturgical dignity of bishops. This panel seems to indicate that the Ruthwell community valued Eucharistic sharing, even when a visiting priest came from a different Christian tradition. Perhaps they were particularly open to friendship with Columban monasteries.

3. Ahenny

From the late 1970s our family set out to add an Irish dimension to Rosemary Cramp's Ruthwell project. Over several summers, we explored most of the Irish crosses. Our children became experts: my daughter was particularly good at finding Adam and Eve panels. These were usually close to the bottom of the cross-shafts (but see section 6, east face). This suited her, because she was aged 3–6 in those years. One day in 1983 we visited the high crosses at Ahenny, Co. Tipperary, near the slopes of Sliabh na mBan. They are perhaps a century later than the Ruthwell Cross. Like the visionary Cross in *The Dream of the Rood* (lines 8–9) both Ahenny crosses have 'five gems up on the shoulder-crossing'. These great bosses, inspired by metalwork, symbolise the five wounds Christ bore on the Cross: four in his hands and feet, and the spear-wound in his side.

We examined the crosses in morning sunshine and began a picnic sitting on the churchyard wall. After the picnic, I had a startling experience looking back at the crosses. Their appearance had changed because the early afternoon sun now shone on them from a different angle. It was clear that these crosses each day gradually revealed new aspects of their symbolism to a community living close to them. They appeared 'living' and 'dynamic' as they interacted with the sun. I resolved to look into how the Irish high crosses, and Ruthwell too, interacted with the sun's course, each day and each season. Hence the title of this lecture, 'Dynamic Theologies'. Monastic stability was a good way to achieve slow, and profound, understanding of chants and monuments. Jennifer O'Reilly has written brilliantly about the cosmic motifs in Irish gospel books,[2] and Hilary Richardson about those of the high crosses. For example, a fourfold image on the north cross at Ahenny affirms the relevance of the four Evangelists and their gospels to the very structure of the universe.

4. Bewcastle

In Northumbria, the damaged eighth-century cross-shaft at Bewcastle, Cumberland is designed to interact with the sun's daily and seasonal course. Its transom and cross-head have been missing since the late sixteenth century; but early antiquaries called it a cross.[3] The cross had plentiful inscriptions, all in runes, some still legible. It was erected out of doors and may have predated the parish church. Its figural panels adapt the complex programme at Ruthwell to commemorate named people.[4]

A roll-moulding frame indicates that each side should be understood as a unity. On the north side the central panel of five is filled with chequers, producing a proliferation of crosses. It is natural, and fascinating, to spend time choosing to switch between interpreting the panel as filled with bright crosses with a dark square at the centre of each, or dark ones with light-filled centres. The other four panels enclose this central one in a double envelope-pattern. 'Insular' interlace fills the flanking panels immediately above and below; they in turn are flanked by large panels of 'continental' vine-scroll motifs. All five panels encourage the onlooker to spend time unravelling their complex intertwining curves. The contrast of styles is perhaps natural near Hadrian's Wall, a cultural borderland. Between each two panels there is a narrow horizontal strip, four on this side and four on the opposite south side: the female name 'kynibur*g' survives in runes above the lower vine-scroll on this side. Other incised or painted names perhaps once existed on some or all of the remaining strips, including 'gess/us' for 'Jesus'. The cross seems designed to commemorate named persons in a Christian context.

---

2 EMTI 1, Chapter 4.

3 R&R, pp. 36–37, fig. 16.

4 This opinion contradicts R&R, pp. 36–47, and, alas, other publications by me.

N
E
S
W

After the spring equinox each year the rising or setting sun gradually begins to shine directly on the north side for a few minutes each morning and evening. As the sun 'goes north' in late March to early June, the slanting rays last longer each dawn and dusk, and cut deeper into the shadows cast by the chequers and other patterns. After the summer solstice, the penetration of the sun's direct rays gradually gets shallower as the sun lessens. People who knew the cross well would have looked forward to the silent yearly message of the north side: that after the equinox, Summer was coming in. Early Christians, building on pre-Christian celebrations of Midwinter and Midsummer, each year celebrated a solar cycle marked out by the births of Christ and his cousin and herald, John the Baptist. They celebrated the conception and birth of Christ, 'the Light of the World', on the sun's 'growing days'. From the late seventh century 'The Annunciation of the Lord', imported to Northumbria from Byzantium via Rome, began to be celebrated on 25 March, just after the spring equinox. His birth on 25 December (the eighth day before the Kalends of January), just after the winter solstice, had already at Rome since the fourth century marked the beginning of winter's defeat by the unconquered sun, 'the light of the world' (John 1:4). Christ's cousin, John the Baptist, 'was not the light, but gave testimony to the light' (John 1:8); speaking of Christ he said, 'he must increase, I must decrease' (John 3:30). John's birth was therefore celebrated on 24 June (the eighth day before the Kalends of July), just after the summer solstice when the sun had begun its decline towards autumn. To complete the solar cycle, John's conception was commemorated on 24 September, just after the autumn equinox. The births of the cousins John and Jesus 'told the seasons', as do the panels of the north side at Bewcastle.

On the east side, the rising sun shines directly on the most beautiful 'continental' vine-scroll to survive from Anglo-Saxon England (adapted from the two earlier versions at Ruthwell, thinner there and provided with runic *tituli*). In seven of its eight volutes, birds and animals joyfully feed on grapes: symbolically they feed on Christ, the vine (John 15:5). Such images, of the Tree of Life in a restored Paradise (Genesis 2:9), were dear to Jennifer O'Reilly since her doctoral days.[5] The great rooted vine-scroll Tree was a

5 Her outstanding doctorate (Nottingham, 1972) was later published: *Studies in the Iconography of the Virtues and Vices in the Middle Ages* (New York, Garland

universal image: recognised and admired by literate and non-literate, Christian and non-Christian alike. An office antiphon for the feasts of the Cross (Finding of the Cross, 3 May; Exaltation of the Cross, 14 September) put the Christian interpretation in plain language or rather plain chant:

> Lignum vitae in cruce tua Domine manifestatum est
> mors enim per ipsam damna est
> et mundus totus per ipsam illuminatus est.
> Omnipotens Domine, gloria tibi.[6]
>
> The Tree of Life has become manifest in your Cross, O Lord;
> death has been condemned by it
> and the whole world is given light by it.
> Omnipotent Lord, Glory to you.

The antiphon provides a clear analogue for the ideas behind the Bewcastle Cross, for example its preoccupation with death and with light. The over-literal translation 'has become manifest' could perhaps be better translated as 'has been revealed'. As we shall see in sections 10 and 12, the antiphon helps us understand the more complex unity of the Ruthwell Cross.

On the south side the double envelope pattern appears again but reversed. A small panel of 'Insular' interlace at the centre of the roll-moulding frame is flanked by two larger panels of 'continental' vine-scroll, which are in turn enclosed by panels of elaborate interlace (the panel at the foot of this side gives a particularly rich blend of cross patterns and 'X' or 'chi' patterns: the 'Chi' was particularly symbolic of Christ's humanity).[7] A sundial is set in the upper vine-scroll. If the north side tells the seasons, this sundial symbolically tells the hours. Its symbolism recalls a central theme of ancient Mass-collects: amidst the distracting variety of life, Christians should fix their hearts on where true happiness may be found.

Immediately to the left sunwise, the guarantors of true happiness are to be found. Each setting sun shines directly on the west side,

---

Publishing, 1988): see especially her Chapter 8.

6 *Corpus Antiphonalium Officii*, No. 3628; search for the *incipit* 'Lignum vitae' at https://gregorien.info.

7 EMTI 1, Chapter 3, pp. 100–106; Chapter 6, pp. 172–186. See section 11 in this memorial lecture.

which has four panels within its roll-moulding frame. A panel of runes is surrounded by three panels with male human figures. All three human figures are accompanied by one or two animals or by a bird. They are adapted from three panels on the second broad side of the Ruthwell Cross. Two panels with arched tops form an envelope pattern around the rectangular panel of runes. The runic panel in turn is visually linked to the rectangular topmost panel. The runic panel begins 'This victory sign [*sigbecn*] was set up by' various named individuals, and ends by asking onlookers to 'pray [*gebid*–] for their souls'. The lowest panel is adapted from the (smaller) panel of John the Evangelist standing to contemplate his eagle on the Ruthwell crosshead. The two panels above the runes represent Christ and John the Baptist, the cousins whose births marked out the seasons. The Bewcastle Cross implies the faith that eternity intersects with the flux of time and gives meaning to it. These panels face west: I shall assume that the corresponding panels at Ruthwell originally faced west also, and give other reasons to think so.

5. Moone, Co. Kildare

The High Cross at Moone is, like Ahenny, a century or more later than Bewcastle. Its slender shaft reminds us of the slender crosses of Northumbria. Several communities of English monks became 'exiles for Christ' in Ireland, so contacts with Northumbria could have been direct.[8] The slender shaft and crosshead contrast with the massive base. While the base situates the Cross at the centre of salvation history, the abstract cosmic images of the shaft and crosshead explore symbolic and cosmic themes, as at Ahenny.

Françoise Henry demonstrated that the base should be read sunwise or *dessel* (Old Irish adverb, 'following one's right hand'). Its epitome of salvation history is revealed each day by the sun's course. It begins on the east. In the narrowing space where base meets shaft, Adam and Eve, about to fall, already flank the tree of the knowledge of good and evil; its abundant apples hang over their backs. The deceiving serpent winds around the tree-trunk, looking expectantly towards Eve. The broader panels just below show a patriarch and a prophet, two heroes to oppose this initial disaster.

8 HHBE, Chapter 1, pp. 20–22; Chapter 5, pp. 136–144.

The Canon of each Mass commemorated 'the sacrifice of our patriarch Abraham': Isaac, a willing son, bends to his father's knife; above and parallel to his bent back the substitute ram already floats. In the lowest scene, the prophet Daniel prays among seven lions.

On the south side, the midday sun shone on the three Jewish boys who (again in the Book of Daniel) sing their canticle in the furnace. A four-winged angel stands protectively over the furnace he has quenched. The curved roof of the furnace allows the central hero to be taller than his flanking fellows as, on the west side, Christ is taller than the flanking thieves: we will become familiar with such 'figure of three' motifs, where the central figure is made known 'in medio duorum', in the midst of two others. The Canticle of the Three Boys called on all creation to praise the Creator: cold or hot, light or dark. This scene is a fitting climax to the Tanakh (Old Testament) sequence on the cross, and a prelude to the two desert scenes below it. In the upper one the baby's head is just visible between his mother Mary (left), and Joseph, who leads the ass: their flight into and return from Egypt had first reversed and then fulfilled the Mosaic exodus. Below them, five loaves and two fishes recall manna, the original desert food, and Christ's feeding of the five thousand. The loaves are flanked by two baton-like monsters, with dogs' ears and heads. These monsters hint that the five loaves between their bodies are sacred, 'known in the midst of two living creatures', though not to be thrown to dogs like them (Matthew 7:6).

Facing the setting sun the second Adam balances the first on the opposite side. Tradition, based loosely on scripture, held that Christ faced west on the Cross, and as far as we can tell the high crosses held faithful to that tradition (of course high crosses could be moved around by later powers that were, powers either unaware or contemptuous of the tradition).[9] Christ on the Cross is flanked by Stephaton the sponge-bearer on his left, and Longinus the spear bearer on his right. It is the moment when Christ's side is pierced and the Church is born from it, symbolised by the water (baptism) and blood (Eucharist), as Eve had been born from the rib from Adam's side, a favourite theme with Jennifer O'Reilly. [10] The Patriarch and

9 The direction west was seen to be 'against the city' of Jerusalem: Romans 10:21 using Isaiah 65:2.

10 EMTI 1, Chapter 1, pp. 34–43, Chapter 6, pp. 169–202; EMTI 2, Chapter 11, pp. 211–213.

Prophet on the east side are here balanced by a single massive block of the twelve apostles, arranged 4x3. The apostles, commanded to take the gospel to the ends of the earth, were rightly emphasised in Ireland, an island behind an island on the edge of Europe. The apostles are severely schematised so that the base appears as a single body with Christ on the Cross as their head: Jennifer O'Reilly wrote with great insight about this theme in the gospel books.[11]

The inauspicious north side carries the story into the monastic present, set like the opposite side in the desert: in Old Irish the loanword *dísert* denoted a monastery or hermitage. Entangled monsters and the desert temptations of St Anthony (to be recognised in the midst of two goat-headed demons) fill the lower space. Where the base narrows towards the shaft Saints Paul and Anthony sit to their meal beneath a lumbering raven. A desert hermitage could become a paradise if humans could learn to live there in harmony with nature. Such an idea may have inspired the vertical row of five animals on the west side of the slender cross-shaft. In Jerome's Life of St Paul, St Anthony the Abbot put the matter baldly: 'wild beasts speak of Christ, while you, city dwellers of Alexandria, worship monsters instead of God.' Alas, idolatry continues. Even in rural Moone it has been necessary to move their cross out of our polluted air. The intended dynamic interplay between salvation history and the sun's course is lost now and for the precarious future.

6. Kells, Market Cross

Kells, Co. Meath, shows that the programmes of crosses could correspond to where in the monastery they were erected. The 'market cross' probably stood near an entrance. Its east side is unified by the idea that Christ is central to the history of salvation. At the crossing, Daniel among two lions again prefigures Christ's triumph between two thieves. The three panels of the shaft are designed to contrast the first Adam with the second (1 Corinthians 15:45–50). The top panel, just under the crossing, unites in a single image the fall of Adam and Eve and its murderous consequence: a towering Cain strikes down a fragile Abel. The lowest panel shows the precise

11 HHBE, Chapter 2; see also EMTI 1, Chapter 3, p. 79, pp. 113–125; and Chapter 6, pp. 186–202.

moment of resurrection on Easter Sunday morning. Christ still lies in his tomb (placed fittingly near the ground); the soldiers still sleep, but they are in for a big surprise (Matthew 28:4). Just outside the tomb, two angels bear between them the tall cross that has spoken to hell to proclaim Christ's victory. It was really tall: its shaft, now interrupted by damage, stretches down between the soldiers' knees; this detail symbolises Christ who was understood to be 'a giant in two natures', as we shall see in the next paragraph. The women approach from the right to anoint Christ's body, but the Spirit is already bringing him back to life (probably: the detail, destroyed on this cross, is found in Irish analogues at Clonmacnoise and Durrow).

The central panel of the shaft unites the first panel (bringers of death, Adam and his sons, above) and the third (the moment of resurrection, below). This panel refers to the sun's course. A giant figure, with spear and shield, advances towards us. Twelve small figures with shields gaze upon him (eight have survived damage). St Augustine, in his commentary on Psalm 18/19, had said that Christ like the sun, proceeding from the bridal chamber of the Virgin's womb (where divinity had been forever wedded to humanity) rejoiced like a giant to run his course. In his Advent hymn, 'Veni Redemptor gentium', St Ambrose called Christ 'geminae gigas substantiae', 'a giant in twin nature' since divinity had become flesh with humanity in the Incarnation. The apostles, here warriors like their Lord, gaze admiringly on his triumphal course. They will announce it even to the ends of the earth, like the apostles at Moone. Monks who joined a monastery like Kells expected that the monastery would be their 'locus resurrectionis', their 'place of resurrection'.[12] These images of resurrection and cosmic triumph summed up what the monastic city was about. On the crossing, the morning sun each day shone on Daniel's survival from between two pairs of lions; the evening sun shone on its fulfilment, the Crucifixion, between Longinus and Stephaton, on the west face.

7. Kells, Cross of the Tower

The 'Cross of Saints Patrick and Columba' or 'Cross of the Tower' apparently stood near a monastic church. The Eucharist is central

12 R&R, pp. 294–298.

to it, unlike the Market Cross. So that the eye can move easily from image to related image, the designer avoided bordered panels. The figures from the Tanakh on the east side of the shaft culminate, just below the crossing, in Daniel between two flanking lions. At the centre of the crossing, seven bosses are displayed on a mat (as it were on a paten). They clearly refer to eucharistic loaves, as they are flanked by 'our father Abraham' sacrificing Isaac (south arm) and Paul and Anthony at table (north arm). Just above the seven bosses, two fishes crossed 'X'-wise provide a *titulus* 'Christ'. The fishes lead our eye to two desert feasts, the seven 'loaves' below them and the five circular 'loaves' just above. The five are placed between David the royal harper-prophet (left) who looks forward to his descendant Christ (right). Christ feeds a multitude (their tiny heads can be seen at the head of the cross). We get a magnificently unified image which combines the feeding in Galilee of the five thousand ('Jews') with two fishes and five loaves (in all four gospels) with the feeding in the Decapolis of a ('gentile') multitude with 'a few fish' and seven loaves (Mark 8:7–10 and Matthew 15:34). The crossed fishes, common to both feasts, act as a transitional image, linking the five loaves (taken to refer to the Pentateuch and so the Jews) to the seven loaves (the seven gifts of the Holy Ghost and so the baptised gentiles). Being crossed 'X'-wise, these fish are not just fish. On the north arm, a pair of book-satchels hang on the arms of the chairs on which Paul and Anthony sit to their meal, a reminder that each Mass also provided two feasts: first intoning and unlocking scripture, then sharing the consecrated loaf and wine. The opposite (west) side juxtaposes Crucifixion to Parousia, the return of Christ in glory. In the Parousia, Christ is revealed, not only as a human figure, but in symbolic form as the Agnus Dei. On the Ruthwell Cross we shall find similar alternation between human and symbolic images of Christ.

8. Muiredach's Cross, Monasterboice, Co. Louth

The east side of Muiredach's Cross spans salvation history, from Adam and Eve with Cain and Abel (at the foot of the shaft) to the return of Christ on Judgement Day at the great wheeled crossing. On the shaft, the designer reverses the course of history, making a theological point in visual terms. Just above the bringers of death, there is hope of a future reversal of the fall and first murder when David triumphs over Goliath in the presence of King Saul and an attendant. To provide a first hint of the very moment of reversal the designer reverses history, bringing us back in time. Moses strikes the rock to provide water for the people of Israel just below the Virgin who at the Epiphany reveals the Christ child to the wise men and their guide. Juxtaposing Moses striking the rock to the Virgin and child made the Epiphany foreshadow the Crucifixion. Christ too would be struck (his side pierced, John 19:34) to provide Baptism and the Eucharist for his people. Just above the head of the baby Jesus is the star which the wise men followed to Bethlehem. But this circular star intersects with the many stars and planets which fill the great wheeled roundel of the cross. When this baby returns as Judge, even the stars will fall from the heavens (Mark 13:25). On the right hand of the majestic Christ at the centre of the crossing, David the harper, his ancestor and greatest of the prophets, advances from the south. David's song is inspired by the dove of the Holy Spirit. A follower bears his prophetic book of psalms; a tiny figure (the commissioner Muiredach) kneels, holding a book, at Christ's right side. David is followed towards Christ by the multitude of the saved. On Christ's left hand, a devil with a pitchfork drives the damned towards the inauspicious north. One heretic bears a banned book. For anyone born in mid-twentieth century Ireland this image is grimly prophetic: then the 'banned book' was a concept all too familiar. This cross is alive with the implied sounds of music, but also with the screeches of the damned. This cross, after all, is tenth century; early Christian art such as the oldest Roman apses, and Ruthwell too, presented the revelation (Parousia) of Christ in glory as an event not to be feared but ardently desired.[13]

After the wide-ranging meditation on salvation history on the east side, we concentrate in the west side on its crucial turning point, Christ's death on the Cross. In the massive Crucifixion scene Longinus (the man with a spear, right) and Stephaton (the sponge-bearer, left) flank Christ. 'Figure of three' or 'in medio duorum' panels, all with Christ at the centre, determine the visual unity of this side. The figure is repeated below in the scenes of arrest, the risen Christ, handing on the law to Peter and Paul, and above in the

13 See EMTI 1, Chapter 1 and Chapter 5; R&R, pp. 228–237, 247–257; figs 41–43, 47–49; plates 9–14.

Ascension. The 'figure of three' is a universal symbol, found for example in native American art, in Tibet, and elsewhere far outside Europe. In ancient court rituals the important figure was honoured by being flanked by lesser figures: the roman term was *sustentatio*, 'supporting'. On the apse of Old Saint Peter's, Rome, Christ was acclaimed and flanked by Saints Peter and Paul (this must have been an unforgettable image for pilgrims). In the Book of Kells 114r, the *sustentatio*-pattern enacted when Christ and two flanking figures 'having sung a hymn, go out towards the Mount of Olivet' marks Christ's solemn entry into his Passion and self-sacrifice.[14] We shall see in section 12 that 'in medio duorum' was central to liturgical commemoration of the moment of Christ's death.

Roger Stalley correctly identified the topmost panel as an Ascension. But it is not just a narrative scene. It takes place in, or in front of, a skeumorphic church or 'temple', a 'Holy of Holies'.[15] Christ's humanity is shown by the wounds visible in his raised hands. He is shown as divine by being 'supported' between two 'Cherubim', a reminder of the pair of cherubim who flank the mercy seat over the Ark of the Covenant (Exodus 25:17–22).[16] With very Irish humour, at the foot of the shaft the commissioner, the abbot Muiredach, appeals for prayers in the midst of two cats, one cherishing, one hunting: 'pray for Muiredach, who had this cross made'. This is the only inscription we have met so far in Ireland. The great Irish crosses didn't need inscriptions: their central scenes portrayed great spans of history familiar to their nuns and monks from celebrating Mass and daily singing of the Psalter and Canticles.

9. Ruthwell, from pillar to cross

Finally, we return to Ruthwell, and from the tenth century back to the eighth. We return from a highly developed tradition to an ambitious and masterly experiment attempting to inaugurate a new one. We go back to the Solway Firth, then Anglo-Saxon territory, but near British and Pictish territories, and near a great Irish monastery, to the

14 EMTI 2, Chapter 5 and Chapter 10.

15 The Tabernacle and the Temple were among Jennifer O'Reilly's major interests: see EMTI 2, Chapter 7, pp. 170–174; HHBE, Chapter 1.

16 HHBE, Chapters 1, 5 and 7; Chapter 2, p. 48; Chapter 8, p. 201; Chapter 12, pp. 301–303.

St John & Eagle
(mistakenly reversed from
second side, see p. 39)

Transom: **Baptism**?
See p. 26

Archer

Visitation

upper stone

Repentance of
Mary Magdalen

Christ heals the man
blind from birth

Annunciation

Crucifixion
(added 9th Century)

Base originally buried

west via an important sea route from the Solway Firth via Whithorn to Bangor, Co. Down.[17] On Ruthwell, there is little apparent interest in the Tanakh or in vast historical patterns, except in one important panel, Christ acclaimed by the beasts.

By the end of the Middle Ages the cross stood within an early (tall and narrow) parish church, but it is likely to have originally stood out of doors for a period, as the Bewcastle Cross still does.[18] When it was moved inside, maybe two or three generations after it was first erected, its massive base did not need to be reburied. In the late eighth or early ninth century a crucifixion panel was added on the first side of the base, just under the Annunciation panel (Annunciation and Crucifixion were believed to have happened on the same day, 25 March[19]). This new panel provided no space for inscription.

The Ruthwell Cross proclaims its romanness, for example in the two 'roman' eagles on its crosshead.[20] Its carving is deep and fairly naturalistic. At the foot of the second broad side the Virgin Mary acclaims her son. On the upper stone, John the Baptist acclaims the Lamb of God. His gesture of acclamation was designed to echo Mary's acclaiming gesture, below at the foot of the shaft. Cousin echoes mother: on both stones acclamation of Christ is, among other perspectives, a family matter. In each of these related panels the two outer legs of the ass (below) and the lamb (above), now knocked off, originally stood free of the background. This aspect of imperial roman sculpture must have impressed early English Rome-pilgrims. Techniques of deep drilling had been lost even in Rome for a century: they were revived there under John VII (pope 705–707) who imported tools, techniques and probably artists from Constantinople.[21] Where did the Ruthwell sculptors get their skills?

All the panels on the cross-shaft are provided with long *tituli*. On the first side of the lower stone, all were direct quotations from the gospels. For an eighth-century religious community this implied chant: scripture was never simply read out in church but always intoned. The Ruthwell Cross implies two kinds of chant: Old Roman

17 R&R, pp. 261–263.
18 R&R, pp. 12–19.
19 R&R, pp. 85–93.
20 R&R, p. 122, pp. 143–146, p. 289; on 'romanitas' cf. EMTI 2, Chapter 4.
21 R&R, pp. 239–247.

chant for some or all of the Latin texts on the broad sides, vernacular song for both *tituli* to the Tree of Life panels. John Osborne has pointed out that to put scriptural quotations on panels was a new idea from Byzantium, first found in Rome in the chapel of John VII. Ruthwell may have been one of the earliest communities to imitate this new practice. Notice the blank space in the lower half of the panel representing the man blind from birth (*De ceco nato*). Was an additional *titulus* attached there to help onlookers interpret the sequence of panels on that first broad side?

Let us imagine the moment when the Ruthwell monument became a cross, that is, when the upper stone was added to the lower. The upper stone is badly damaged, probably when it was pulled down by iconoclasts in 1641. The colour of its sandstone is darker than the lower stone, but such variations can occur even in the same quarry. The variation would not have been visible if, as seems likely, the cross was given a gesso undercoat and painted.[22] The upper stone may have been added a few days after the lower stone was erected; or maybe a year or two had passed. Perhaps a different sculptor from the same school was engaged. It is likely that there was time for the community to do some creative rethinking, for example whether they might vary the placing of runes and roman script in order to complement the iconography of the stone. The upper stone completes and unifies the programme of the lower: the monument was planned from the beginning as a complex and highly coherent cross.

The first broad side of the damaged upper stone had two sections: the large Visitation panel, and the crosshead. The latter is fragmented (the present transom is a nineteenth century substitute). Each broad side comprised five sections: three on the lower stone, two on the upper. In the gospel of Luke, the Annunciation and Visitation episodes follow each other directly (Luke 1:26–38, 39–56). One phrase, 'blessed art thou among women', is common to both, with a verbal variant: Gabriel says 'in mulieribus' (1:28) but Elizabeth says 'inter mulieres' (1:42). Directly after the Annunciation, Mary headed off into the hill country to help her elderly cousin Elizabeth: Gabriel had just told Mary that Elizabeth was six months with child. On Mary's arrival, Elisabeth's unborn son leaped in her womb to

22 R&R, pp. 27–32.

acclaim Jesus in Mary's womb. Liturgical uses associated the two lections even more intimately. The Annunciation lection (Luke 1:26–38) was intoned on Ember Wednesday in December. Ember week began after St Lucy's day on 13 December, and usually coincided with the third week of Advent. The Visitation lection (Luke 1:39–56) was intoned two days later, on Ember Friday. The Offertory chant at the Wednesday Mass combined Gabriel's greeting (expanding the phrase 'Ave gratia plena' in Luke 1:28 to 'Ave Maria gratia plena' and using Gabriel's variant 'in mulieribus') with part of Elizabeth's: 'et benedictus fructus ventris tui' ('and blessed is the fruit of your womb', Luke 1:42). This extended chant was also sung the following Sunday, the fourth of Advent and last before Christmas. The gospel lection Luke 26–38 and the Offertory chant 'Ave Maria' had from the late seventh century begun also to be chanted on the new feast of the Annunciation (25 March).[23]

Once the upper stone was in place, the Visitation panel with the Annunciation below enveloped the two panels between them as in a womb. Those who performed a local liturgy based on that of eighth-century Rome would not have found this metaphor strange or indecorous. On Holy Thursday, both catechumens and penitents were encouraged to see the Church as a pregnant mother, anxious to bring them to new birth or rebirth in time for Easter: 'now having conceived you the pregnant Church rejoices'; and similar images recurred in the solemn blessing of the font for baptisms on the Easter vigil.[24] The *tituli* of the three panels on this first side of the lower stone quoted the *incipits* or opening verses of gospel lections chanted on specific days. The curing of the man blind from birth and the forgiveness of the weeping woman 'because she had loved much' clearly celebrate faith and repentance. These lections were intoned at Lenten Masses which prepared for ceremonies of repentance and reconciliation (the 'scrutiny' ceremonies) and for Baptism on the Vigil of Easter.[25] To place these panels between Annunciation and Visitation was to link Lenten repentance and spiritual growth unforgettably to Christ's Incarnation and growth towards birth in Mary's womb. Once the upper stone completed the cross, no member of the Ruthwell community was likely to forget

23 R&R, pp. 95–99, p. 357.
24 R&R, p. 137.
25 R&R, pp. 126–137.

that Christ's Incarnation was fundamental to spiritual growth as well as to their communal participation in the yearly Lenten liturgy. Through baptism, Christians were expected to become bearers of Jesus Christ like Mary, mother of God.[26]

10. The upper stone and the first broad side

Placing the upper stone completed the Annunciation-Visitation 'envelope pattern'. It also made the third panel, 'the woman who was a sinner', central to the first broad side. On the authority of Gregory the Great (pope 590–604), who was followed by many writers including Bede, Northumbrian Christians identified this woman with Mary Magdalen, whom Christ praised while contrasting her to his face in conversation with Simon, a judgemental and self-righteous Pharisee: 'her sins which were many are forgiven, for she loved much. But to a person to whom little is forgiven loves little' (Luke 7:47). Her compassionate love for Christ's humanity, symbolised by her tears at and care for his feet, was the turning point in a great spiritual biography. She would later come to anoint his head (symbol of his divinity); she would be one of the three Marys standing by the Cross; and on Easter morning Christ in the garden would, calling her by her name, send Mary as 'apostle to the apostles' to announce to them that he had risen.[27] Katherine Ludwig Jansen has termed Gregory's highly influential exegesis 'audacious but not capricious', and Sr Benedicta Ward has shown that Gregory gathered together scattered references in the gospels to women named 'Mary' in order to show that there was another road to the heights of contemplation, different from but complementary to that offered to, and chosen by, Mary of Nazareth.[28] Mary Magdalen's penitential path to holiness was closer to normal Christian experience than that of the mother of God. As we shall see, by Bede's time Gregory's pastorally creative idea had come to be confirmed by liturgical use.

Lent, the 'lengthening' season when the sun triumphs over winter darkness, was seen, like ember days, to be a 'sacrament' (*sacramentum*) bringing those who practised it deeper into

26 R&R, pp. 138–140.

27 R&R, pp. 132–137. The title 'apostle to the apostles' began to be used in the twelfth century.

28 Quoted at R&R, p. 136.

mysterium Christi, the mystery of Christ.[29] Lent involved a series of ceremonies in which the infant catechumens were examined (the ceremonies were therefore called 'scrutinies'), exorcised from traces of demonic possession, and instructed, via their godparents and families, in the basic documents of the faith. The Our Father, the Apostles' Creed and the four Gospels (their *incipits* explained with reference to their Evangelist symbols), were symbolically 'passed on' to the little catechumens, in the persons of their godparents and families.[30]

Lent culminated in the Easter Triduum, the three days from Friday to Sunday of Holy Week, when the community participated in Christ's death, victory over Satan, and resurrection. The climax was the Vigil of Easter on Holy Saturday night. The vigil began with a series of intoned readings, first from the Tanakh (Genesis, Exodus, Prophets) and then from the New Testament. The relevance of each reading was summed up, and interpreted in public prayers, to be a *mysterium*, a pattern of history leading to the *mysterium* of Christ. The readings ended with a resurrection narrative (Matthew 28:1–7). After this meditation on the shape of history came the baptisms. The Easter Vigil was seen as the ideal time for baptism: the descent into and emergence from the baptismal font (even if, for infant baptism in eighth century Northumbria, it was reduced to pouring water over the neophyte's head) was understood to be a participation in Christ's death, burial and resurrection.[31] Baptisms led directly to the vigil Mass of Easter, and reception of the Eucharist by the newly baptised, infants though they usually were.[32] Lent was at this period seen as a preparation (for all, not only for the neophytes) for the rituals of the Easter Vigil. These rituals formed a unified sequence (Lenten conversion and spiritual growth, leading to Baptism and culminating in reception of the Eucharist). That unity is an important key to understanding the unity of the Ruthwell Cross: growth towards baptism for the first broad side, recognition of Christ and reception of him in the Eucharist, for the second.

The Visitation panel, which closes the 'envelope', emphasises pregnancy and new life. Elizabeth (on the right) explores the

29 R&R, pp. 120–126; EMTI 1, Chapter 5, pp. 153–160; Chapter 6, pp. 179–180.

30 R&R, pp. 126–137.

31 EMTI 1, Chapter 5, pp. 143–151.

32 R&R, p. 126, p. 148.

womb of Mary, who encourages the intimate womanly gesture by embracing Elizabeth's upper arm. The scene is set just after Elizabeth's son John has leapt in her womb to acknowledge the presence of the Messiah. Elizabeth stares towards Mary, but Mary turns her head partially towards the onlookers. This is the moment when she intoned the *incipit* of her 'Magnificat' (Luke 1: 46–55), the canticle sung each evening at Vespers. The east side of the cross, lit by each rising sun, thus anticipates the daily chant which, as Bede put it, enabled the community each evening to compose their minds after the day's distractions.[33] The moment Mary begins to sing her Magnificat is represented as precisely as the moment of resurrection on the Market Cross at Kells (see section 6).

Just above the Visitation panel an archer, in high relief, draws his bow. Around his neck he wears a book-satchel (we saw such satchels on the Cross of the Tower at Kells, cf. section 7). The open satchel contains a rectangular object, like a book. Archers were seen to symbolise preachers, who shoot the words of scripture at the hearts of their congregations.[34] Isaiah 49:1–2 began with a theme so central to Jennifer O'Reilly's teaching and scholarship that Diarmuid Scully and Elizabeth Mullins named her Festschrift after its *incipit* 'Listen, O Isles, unto me'.[35] Isaiah referred to himself as 'a chosen arrow, hidden in God's quiver' (49:2). Christian commentary saw Christ as the uniquely 'chosen arrow'; he was hidden in God's quiver when, at his Incarnation, his divinity was hidden in a human body and nature. The liturgy, however, celebrated one exception to the identification of the chosen arrow with Christ. At Mass on the Nativity of John the Baptist (24 June), the Introit chant and the Old Testament lection, both, were taken from Isaiah 49:1–2. It is as if John got a midsummer birthday present. John too could be said to be the 'chosen arrow hidden in God's quiver' because at the Visitation he was still hidden in his mother's womb when he first proclaimed Jesus as Messiah. At the Visitation Christ and John were both hidden chosen arrows. Scribes at Wearmouth added one of their very rare notes in the Codex Amiatinus to mark out Isaiah 49:1 as special: 'in sci ioh bap' (fol. 526r),'on [the feast] of St John the Baptist'.

33 R&R, p. 310.
34 R&R, pp. 141–143.
35 HHBE, Chapters 2 and 4.

The *titulus* to the Visitation panel, indeed all the surviving inscriptions on this first side of the upper stone, are in runes. The designer used these runes iconographically to connote 'hidden mystery': the English word 'rune' was taken into Old Irish before the end of the eighth century to mean 'secret'. In contrast, on the second broad side of this upper stone, where the adult John the Baptist openly acclaims Christ as the Agnus Dei, the *titulus* and other inscriptions are in roman capitals, the official script of the Church and its liturgy. What here is hidden there becomes publicly proclaimed. As an adult John fulfilled the prophecy his father Zachary had made about him: 'you will become the prophet of the most High' (Luke 1:78). This panel faced west: for nuns or monks at Ruthwell its image of John, prophet of Christ's sacrificial death as Lamb of God, anticipated the next sunrise, when their community would sing Zachary's canticle the 'Benedictus'. Zachary's son John the Baptist would prepare the way for Christ, the morning star, bringer of light to those 'who sit in darkness and the shadow of death' (Luke 1: 68–79). The two large panels of the upper stone reflect the unity of the monastic day by recalling the two canticles which gave it spiritual shape. The panels counterpoint the physical growth of John and Jesus from the Visitation (east) to the Agnus Dei (west) against daily monastic prayer, from the sunrise Benedictus at Lauds (west) to the evening Magnificat at Vespers (east): the sun shone *behind* the images referring to the canticles sung at these hours. This created a daily counterpoint between the lives of the two cousins, the daily monastic canticles, and the sun's course. The Visitation panel on the east side of the Ruthwell Cross in addition recalls the yearly solar cycle. In the days close to 24 June, it would have been natural to pay attention to Elizabeth (on the right), pregnant with John. She faces south, the direction taken by the lessening sun each autumn. At midwinter it would have been natural to pay attention to Mary (on the left). She faces north, the direction taken by the growing sun each spring. The upper stone at Ruthwell celebrates the sun's daily and seasonal course as does Bewcastle.[36] Such rich reference at Ruthwell to the monastic day may have inspired the simpler but evocative symbolic sundial at Bewcastle. It would not have been practical to depend on the slowly-shifting shadow of the Bewcastle

36 R&R, pp. 106–107.

sundial to know the times when services began. However in a parish or settlement served by 'secular' clergy it may have helped to remind clergy and laity that the Passion had daily 'hours'. The gospels, in their accounts of Christ's crucifixion, mention the third (Mark 15:25), sixth (Mark 15:33) and ninth (Mark 15:34) hours.[37] Clergy might well have recommended that laity, even if they did not formally chant 'terce', 'sext' or 'nones', might pause at about these hours, roughly indicated by the sundial, to recollect the Passion, or for moments of private prayer between more formal prayers at morning (Lauds) and evening (Vespers).

The lower half of the Ruthwell Visitation panel is severely damaged.[38] Reading downwards on the right border the *incipit* of an inscription is signalled by a little cross: '+ dominnæ c –'. The rest of this statement about 'ladies' or 'women' is destroyed. Reading upwards on the left border the word '– marþ[a]' comes just above the damage. Perhaps that damaged border originally read '[maria et] marþ[a]': a phrase beginning with 'Maria' would have linked this panel firmly to the moving portrait of Mary Magdalen just below. The runes on the top border perhaps read 'mar[ia] m[ate]r', 'Mary the mother'. To judge by these scattered fragments and their placing, the *titulus* seems to place 'dominnae' such as 'Mary the mother' (she certainly is a pregnant mother in the Visitation panel) and Elizabeth among other women, perhaps especially Mary [Magdalen] and Martha of Bethany. The runic *titulus* may possibly have been inspired by Elizabeth's echo of Gabriel's acclamation 'blessed art thou among women', fragments of which ('T*E*cum B*E*nedicta') survive on the left margin of the Annunciation panel below. Runes placed so high up were never easy to read as a connected statement or statements. But concepts such as 'Incarnation', 'mystery' and 'blessed among women' were important to a monastic community. We have seen that the Annunciation and Visitation lections were intoned several times each year, as was the Offertory chant which linked them verbally. It was easy, by merely pointing, to remind anyone that the 'blessed among women' of the Annunciation panel also applied to the Visitation panel above. The two *tituli*, roman and runic, certainly reinforced the strong visual and aural links already forged between the two scenes.

37 Cf. also Matthew 27:45 and parallels.

38 R&R, pp. 103–106.

We have seen that the Virgin Mary and Mary Magdalen were closely associated ever since Gregory the Great unified various namesakes of Mary in the gospels to compile his 'biography' of the Magdalen. By Bede's time liturgical use had strongly confirmed the association. In the new Marian feasts, the Visitation became the gospel lection for the Nativity of the Virgin Mary (8 September). The Martha and Mary of Bethany lection (Luke 10:38–42) was intoned three weeks earlier, as the Gospel for the new feast of the Virgin Mary's Dormition (her death or *natale*, entry into heaven, 15 August). That feast (later known as her Assumption) was the most important of the four Marian feasts introduced from Byzantium to Rome, and thence to Northumbria, in the seventh and early eighth centuries. The death or dormition of the Virgin did not feature in the canon of scripture to be intoned in church. Instead, on that day the roman liturgy proclaimed that the Virgin 'Mary has taken the better part, and it shall not be taken from her' (cf. Luke 10:42). This startlingly close identification of the two Marys tells us a lot about how both Marys were seen at that period. If Christ's affirmation of the contemplative Mary Magdalen (identified with Mary of Bethany) was intoned as gospel on the day when his mother Mary entered heaven, that implied that the Virgin, by her own choice ('fiat', Luke 1:38), had become the greatest of contemplatives when she chose to become mother of God Incarnate without male seed, 'sine virili semine'.[39] Both the iconographic sequence and the fragmentary runic *titulus* suggest familiarity with the new Marian feasts. Similarly, the decision to place the archer just above the Visitation panel, implying that both babies in their mothers' wombs are 'chosen arrows, hidden in God's quiver', indicates familiarity (as at Wearmouth) with the Nativity of John the Baptist. Runic reconstructions are always speculative, particularly when the runes are fragmentary, scattered, possibly allusive, and placed high up. But the upper stone not only completes the Ruthwell Cross: it contains some of its richest liturgical symbolism. The first broad side, centred on the moving image of Mary Magdalen responding to Christ's humanity, affirms love, forgiveness, choice, life and contemplation. It rebukes the misuse of the name 'Magdalen' in recent Irish history as a front for hypocritical exclusion, self-righteous discrimination,

39 R&R, p. 288 'sine semine', and p. 322; cf. Ambrose 'Veni Redemptor gentium', strophe 5; see section 6 (Kells, Market Cross).

and loveless cruelty. Jesus' rebuke of Simon the Pharisee to his face in Luke 7:47 remains all too relevant.

We might expect the four-panel envelope pattern, closely associating the Virgin Mary's pregnancy with the Lenten 'pregnancy' of the Church, to culminate in an image of birth. But we now have only fragments of the crosshead. There is no Nativity scene on the cross. But baptism was itself seen as a virgin birth without male seed. At a sermon in St Peter's on Christmas Morning AD 444 Leo I (pope 440–461) gave that idea classic formulation:

> He [Christ] placed in the font of Baptism that very origin which he had assumed in the Virgin's womb. He gave to the water what he had given to his Mother. For the same power of the Most High and overshadowing of the Holy Spirit [Luke 1:35] that caused Mary to bear the Saviour makes the water regenerate the believer.[40]

The iconoclasts in 1641 did a fairly efficient job of destroying the crosshead; nevertheless the Rev. Henry Duncan was able in 1823 to preserve its lower and upper arms: archer below, eagle above.[41] Building on his careful work, in wartime (1943) a great German scholar, Fritz Saxl of the Warburg Institute (a tabernacle of interdisciplinary scholarship much frequented and admired by Jennifer O'Reilly) suggested that the Ruthwell crosshead may have indirectly inspired (perhaps via Lindisfarne) three fragmentary crossheads from Durham. These certainly provide a good analogue for the Ruthwell eagle above the transom. Their eagles too seem to have turned their beaks towards the rock (one of these eagles survives, and the tail of a second).[42] They are late, from the eleventh century; but Ruthwell parish was dedicated to St Cuthbert whose cult after Lindisfarne centred on Durham. The transoms of the Durham crossheads represent Lenten scrutinies and Easter baptism. On all three crossheads a scene of baptism in the central roundel is flanked by mirrored scenes of a catechumen being 'scrutinised' by clerics bearing books and crosses. The Ruthwell archer aims his arrows at the right arm of the transom, probably at a 'scrutinised' catechumen.

40 R&R, p. 139; pp. 120–140.
41 R&R, pp. 21–23.
42 R&R, p. 146 and fig. 30(a)–(c).

The archer, like the crossed fishes on the Kells Cross of the Tower (see section 7), is a transitional image, linking the Visitation, the moment when Incarnation was first acclaimed, to preaching and instruction (in the scrutinies), necessary preludes to the birth of baptism (perhaps on the central roundel of the transom). Saxl's theory that the Durham crossheads provide an analogue for the missing transom supports the arguments for a Lindisfarne connection put forward most recently by Claire Stancliffe (there is no reason to believe that the Lindisfarne connection was exclusive).[43]

The eagle on the upper arm provides another remarkable transition. It stands with its left leg on the topmost branch of a 'vine-tree'. Its right leg is raised, as though preparing to take flight. Its head is turned to its right, so that its hooked beak is limned against the 'rock' of the crosshead. Psalm 102/3:5 refers to an ancient legend. As it grows old, the hooked beak of the eagle grows down over its lower beak. No longer able to eat, it begins to die of hunger. It can only eat when it rubs away its hook on the rock. Then its youth is renewed. Patristic commentary identified the rock with Christ, and the Eagle's hunger with desire for the Eucharist.[44] The Ruthwell community would have sung Psalm 102/3 weekly. Its opening verses (1–5) provided the libretto for the Offertory chant at Mass on

43 R&R, pp. 54–8, 282–285, 298–299.
44 R&R, pp. 143–146.

Friday of the first week in Lent, an ember week. Ember weeks are important to this broad side: it was during ember week in Advent that the Annunciation and Visitation were intoned. During ember weeks parishes went in procession to pray for fertility and growth of the spring crops. The Offertory chant stressed the importance of gratitude:

> Benedic anima mea dominum, et noli oblivisci omnes retributiones eius
> […] ut renovabitur sicut aquilae iuventus tua. (verses 1 and 5)
>
> My soul, bless the Lord, and do not forget all his kindnesses
> […] so that your youth will be renewed like the eagle's.

The Offertory, stressing gratitude for renewed life, brings the theme of this whole first broad side to a fitting climax. When the Eagle has rasped away its hooked beak on the rock, it will be hungry: the panel looks forward to the Eucharist, the central issue in the second broad side. The Easter Vigil rites of initiation always culminated in the Eucharist, difficult though it must have been to administer under both species, bread and wine, to little babies. The rites of reception into monastic communities, both in the eastern and western Churches, were modelled on those of Christian initiation.[45] They too involved 'scrutinies' to determine suitability, solemn vows, clothing with a new habit, and finally participation in a communal Eucharist. The Ruthwell Cross was as relevant to nuns or monks as to the laity. A monastic community was designed to help its members become Christian, living out in their vow of *conversatio morum* ('to pay attention to their way of life') what baptism demanded of all Christians.[46]

This first side presents a unified image of growth towards birth and renewed life. The central image of its five sections, the tearful turning point in the loving life of Mary Magdalen, is enclosed in a double envelope–pattern. The inner envelope balances Christ's compassionate healing of the man born blind (below) with the Visitation (above). The Lenten lection *De Ceco nato* (John 9:1–41), told of a new creation. The Ruthwell panel vividly portrays Christ

45 R&R, pp. 294–296.
46 R&R, pp. 292–297; HHBE, Chapter 3, pp. 80–87.

using a stick to daub the man's blind eyes with mud he has spat on. Adam was created from mud: here Christ moistens the mud with his own spittle, an intimate image of humanity and grace. Christ tells the slowly healing blind man to wash, as in baptism; the man begins gradually to comprehend Christ's humanity and finally his divinity. Christ debates with the spiritually blind Pharisees who refused to see that he is the light of the world (John 9:5). The envelope pattern matches *De ceco nato* with the Visitation, where two eloquent far-seeing women celebrate the two coming births that will transform the world. The Annunciation at the foot of the shaft not only inaugurates the iconographic programme spanning both broad sides; it also inaugurates the outer 'envelope' pattern spanning this side. This vitally important 'envelope' links the moment of Incarnation at the Annunciation to the (hypothetical) image of baptism on the transom. Baptism was understood as a new birth from the virginal womb of the font. As we have seen, the neophytes were also understood to participate in Christ's death and resurrection: in the baptismal font they died to their previous life, and then rose from that virginal womb to share in the life of the Trinity.[47]

11. The Tree of Life panels and their *tituli*

The narrow sides are filled with twin images of the Tree of Life. Jennifer O'Reilly argued eloquently that the Tree was central to the cross.[48] By means of their vernacular runic *tituli* these panels give the audience the perspective they need to understand the iconographic programmes of the broad sides to their left (sunwise or *dessel*: see section 5, Moone). The heroic narrative of each vernacular *titulus* provides urgent motivation to respond to the images sunwise or *dessel* in relation to it. Jennifer O'Reilly's classic analysis of the *tituli* on the Durham Gospels Crucifixion page has given us a sophisticated model for analysing the even longer Ruthwell *tituli*.[49] Like the Durham Gospels image all the surviving Ruthwell *tituli* are masterly examples of ekphrasis (spelling out the significance of a work of art). The Ruthwell runic verse *tituli* are in addition

47 R&R, pp. 146–147; EMTI 1, Chapter 5, pp. 143–151; EMTI 2, Chapter 7, pp. 162–165; HHBE, Chapter 5, pp. 117–120.

48 EMTI 2, Chapter 3, p. 59, quoted R&R, p. 286; R&R, pp. 47–50 and pp. 285–287.

49 EMTI 1, Chapter 5.

outstanding examples of prosopopeia, in which a work of art, in this case the cross, narrates its own experience.

The runes are carefully edited onto four columns. Their layout resembles that of the Latin verse *titulus* to the icon of Santa Maria in Trastevere. Pope John VII had his portrait painted kneeling at the foot of the Virgin in that icon, and recent scholarship tends to conclude that the whole icon may have been painted in his short reign (705–07).[50] Each column may have comprised a self-contained *sententia* or unit of meaning: we can't know this for sure, as the end of each column is damaged. The damaged spaces, even if filled with runes, would have had room for just one two-stress verse (half-line) at the bottom of each of three columns. On Column III, two runes of what looks like the final phrase of the third *sententia* survive, and that verse has been reconstructed from the Vercelli *Dream* (59b). The four columns provide a simple guide to the whole cross, because to read them in sequence we must move around the cross sunwise or *dessel*.[51] This gives the *tituli* to the Tree of Life a unique structural importance, and not only among the Ruthwell *tituli*. On no other surviving object from Anglo-Saxon England are runes fundamental to the structure of such original and profound theological thought.

The designer provided for each *titulus* a memorable *incipit*. They are easy to read and remember, because they run horizontally across the top of each narrow side of the lower stone and end in the right-hand column. This makes it obvious that the right-hand columns are to be read first, then the left-hand columns, as in the Roman icon of Santa Maria in Trastevere.[52] A *punctum* marks off the end of each *incipit*. Both function like modern headlines, making each *titulus* into a visual unit and stating its central theme. The first *incipit* (north) makes a lapidary statement about the kenosis of God the Son:

> **[+ ond]ġeredæ hinæ god almehttiġ .**
> Almighty God stripped Himself.

This is not based on a gospel narrative: nowhere do the four gospels say that Jesus stripped himself before being crucified. Instead, it

50 R&R, pp. 240–241 and plate 8.
51 R&R, p. 261.
52 R&R, p. 241.

paraphrases the classic description of divine kenosis, where Jesus, being equal to God, 'stripped himself' or 'emptied himself' of divine glory ('*exinanivit seipsum*') and 'revealed himself' to us in taking human form, 'the form of a slave' (Philippians 2:7).[53] The *incipit*, summing up what Incarnation meant, refers primarily to the moment Incarnation and kenosis began, the Annunciation. After the *punctum*, the runic *titulus* will describe the Crucifixion; but not until after that point.

If the first *incipit* (facing north) epitomised divine kenosis, the second epitomises how, when kenosis was completed and Christ slept in death, the Cross cared for the body of the dead hero. The Cross still exalts and is united to his corpse:

> **[+] kris[t] wæs on rōdi .**
> + Christ was on the Cross.

To modern readers this *incipit* might appear banal: we use title 'Christ' casually, even to swear. But Jennifer O'Reilly has demonstrated, in her analyses of the great pages which Insular gospel books devote to the symbol 'chi–rho' ('*Xp*', i.e. the first letters in the Greek alphabet of the word 'Christ'), that early Insular monastic communities had a quite different attitude to the title 'Christus' ('the anointed one', 'the Messiah', 'the King of the Jews') than we are likely to have. The 'chi-rho' pages illuminated the initial letters of the initial word of Matthew 1:18, '***Chr***isti autem generatio sic erat': 'this was the generation of ***Chr***ist'. They are a major feature of early Insular gospel books, but not of continental ones. At Matthew 1:18 Christ's paternal genealogy (down to Joseph) was interrupted by the Virgin Birth.[54] The Holy Spirit and the power of the Most High, not Joseph, begat Jesus. In the 'chi-rho' pages Insular artists celebrated the moment when in the thalamus or bridal chamber of Mary's womb God became one flesh with humankind. If the first Ruthwell *incipit* epitomised Jesus' kenotic divinity, the second fixes our attention on how the Cross took care of Christ's human and vulnerable corpse.

Now we shall examine what, after its *incipit*, each *titulus* goes on to say:

53 R&R, pp. 164–166.

54 EMTI 1, Chapter 3, pp. 80–88; EMTI 2, Chapter 7, pp. 186–189, Chapters 8 and 9.

The *titulus* to the first Tree of Life panel (facing north)

***Incipit* and Column I (top and right-hand border)**

1a **[+ ond]ġeredæ hinæ god almehttiġ .**
1b þā hē walde on galgu ġistīga
2 mōdiġ f[oræ] [allæ] men
3 [b]ūg[a iċ ni dorstæ] {...}

1a **[+] God Almighty stripped himself .**
1b When he resolved to mount the gallows,
2 courageous [before all] men,
3 Be[nd I did not dare] {...}.

Its *incipit* epitomised divine kenosis; the rest of the first *titulus* develops the idea. It sings a new song, reshaping the Crucifixion narrative to recall the Incarnation, the moment kenosis began. This narrative is not based on the gospels: all four of them tell that Jesus carried his Cross to Calvary. Instead, it imagines the Cross as already standing in position in an unspecified place. This makes the narrative more immediate: might it be devotionally appropriate to imagine that it happened at Ruthwell itself, here where the cross stands? The Cross is confronted by a heroic Christ resolved to ascend it. Jesus' act of will ('wolde', 1b, 'resolved') is a divine act: 'he' of line 1b refers back to 'god almehttiġ' of the *incipit*. It is also a human act: the phrase 'modig fore allæ men' means both 'braver than all other men' and 'brave in the sight of all men'. Lines 1b–2 are as close as narrative poetry can get to paraphrasing the decree of the Lateran Council of 649 that Christ 'wills and effects our salvation at once divinely and humanly'. This line and a half (1b–2) is a vernacular epitome of the central argument for the western rejection of Monotheletism.[55]

Such a confrontation had already happened at the Annunciation, as any monastic audience would have remembered. The Crucifixion was believed to have taken place on 25 March, the anniversary of the Annunciation.[56] Angels had names that recalled their most important intervention in human history: 'Gabriel' meant 'fortitudo Dei', 'the courage [or strength] of God': Gregory the Great, followed by Bede

55 R&R, pp. 81–83; HHBE, Chapter 6.
56 R&R, pp. 83–106.

and many others, explained why Gabriel was sent at the Incarnation:

> And therefore to the Virgin Mary is sent Gabriel, who is called 'the courage of God' [*fortitudo Dei*] because he came to announce Him who deigned to appear, humble, to defeat the powers of the air ['*qui ad debellandas aereas potestates humilis uenire dignatus est*']. About him it is said by the Psalmist, 'Lift up your gates, o ye princes, and be lifted up, o eternal gates: and the King of Glory shall come in.' Who is this king of glory? The Lord who is strong and mighty, the Lord mighty in battle [Psalm 23/24:7–8] and again, 'The Lord of Hosts, he is the King of Glory' [Psalm 23/24:10]. He was therefore to be announced by the courage of God who, Lord of Hosts and powerful in battle, came to make war against the powers of the air [*qui uirtutum Dominus et potens in proelio, contra potestates aereas ad bella ueniebat*].[57]

The *incipit* and first column already make it clear that Jesus' heroic resolve to ascend the Cross completed his initial kenotic choice to become human. If Mary showed courageous obedience in agreeing to provide the Word of God with a human body and nature ('fiat mihi', Luke 1:38), the Cross now shows heroic obedience by bearing him to his death. It is likely that this theme was announced towards the end of this column. Two runes from a damaged word survive, and on the basis of *Dream* 43b scholars have reconstructed the phrase as '[b]ūg[a iċ ni dorstæ]' (3). The idea is (re)iterated in the left-hand column ('hælda iċ ni dorstæ' (5b): 'I dared not bend'). Unlike Mary, the Cross could not speak when confronted with the courage of Christ; but it now sings as the Tree of Life, revealed in the Cross.[58]

Column II (left-hand border)

4 [hōf] iċ rīcnæ Kyniŋc .
5 heafunæs hlāfard hælda iċ ni dorstæ
6 [bi]smæræ[d]u uŋKet men bā ætgad[re] iċ [wæs] [m]iþ
b[l]ōdæ bistēmi[d]
7 bi[goten of þæs gumu sīda] {… }

57 R&R, pp. 84–85.
58 Cf. section 4, the antiphon 'Lignum vitae in cruce tua'.

4 I [lifted up] the Mighty King:
5 the Lord of Heaven I dared not bend.
6 They mocked the pair of us both together: I [was] drenched with blood
7 po[ured from the man's side.] {...}

In the second column the Cross not only reiterates its obedience (5b) but tells us that it exalted Jesus, revealing him as 'a powerful king, the Lord of heaven'(4–5). Jennifer O'Reilly has written an important study on the wounded and exalted Christ.[59] It was when Jesus 'humbled himself and became obedient to the point of death – even death on a cross' that 'God exalted him, and gave him the name [Jesus] that is above every other name' (Philippians 2:8–9). The gospel of John presents the Crucifixion as already Jesus' exaltation. The Cross reveals Christ's divine kingship to all the world 'so that at the name of Jesus every knee should bow' (Philippians 2:10). The heroism they share unites the Cross with Christ.[60]

They are also closely united by the mockery aimed at both (6a). We are not told who the mockers are. Reflective nuns or monks would have seen their own unworthy actions as mocking Christ.[61] Cross and Christ are further united when the Cross is drenched by Christ's blood. The Gospel of John uniquely relates that one of the Roman soldiers 'opened his side with a spear, and at once blood and water came out' (19:34). As we have seen (see section 5, Moone), Patristic and Insular traditions alike proclaimed that at this moment the Church and her sacraments were born from Christ's side, as Eve had been born from Adam's.[62]

The Tree of Life sings in the persona of the Cross. Its new vernacular song was shaped to give singers, hearers and onlookers precisely the perspective they needed to understand the iconographic sequence on the first broad side, to which it led sunwise or *dessel*. The vernacular *titulus* profoundly unifies this first half of the cross, so that the narrow and broad sides, read in sequence, make the first major statement in Insular culture that God and humans are united by gift-

59 EMTI 1, Chapter 1.
60 R&R, pp. 93–94.
61 R&R, pp. 80–81.
62 R&R, p. 81; EMTI 1, Chapter 6, p. 172; EMTI 2, Chapter 11, p. 212.

exchange (we will soon meet the second).[63] The Tree of Life's song recalls that divine kenosis began at the Annunciation: Mary's 'fiat' permitted God the Son to receive in her womb his human body and nature, including his human will. Her gift added to his pre-existing divine nature and participation in the divine will. Henceforth, thanks to her 'fiat', he would be 'a giant in two natures' (see section 6). The Cross, loyally bearing him to his heroic death, enabled him to complete a lifelong kenosis that began at his conception. Christ grew to birth in the thalamus (bridal chamber) of Mary's womb so that humans, henceforth 'two in one flesh' with him (Genesis 2:23–24), could grow via baptism towards deeper participation in his divine life. This provided the audience with urgent motivation to respond to what Tree-Cross and iconographic sequence together proclaimed, through images explained in two languages, two scripts and two traditions of song. Through its English vernacular *titulus* the Tree of Life sings a new song to show that kenosis unified Christ's life, from Incarnation to the Cross. The layout of the *titulus* leads onlookers or audience *dessel*, sunwise to where, through the Cross, growth and life take place in the sacraments of Lent and Baptism. 'God almighty stripped himself' (1a) of his divine glory and endured the cross so that his human brothers and sisters, thankful when in baptism their life is renewed like the eagle's, could through the Eucharist share with him in the life of the Trinity.

The *titulus* to the second Tree of Life panel (facing south)
***Incipit* and Column III (top and right-hand border)**

8 **[+] kris[t] wæs on rōdi .**
9 hweþræ þēr fūsæ fearran kwōmu
10 æþþilæ til ānum iċ þæt al bi[heald]
11 sā[ræ] iċ w[æ]s . mi[þ] so[r]gu[m] ġidrœ̄[fi]d h[n]āg [iċ þām seċgum til handa]

8 **[+] Christ was on the Cross:**
9 however, eagerly there came from afar
10 noble ones to the [special] one. I beheld it all.
11 I was terribly . afflicted with sorrows: I bo[wed to the men's hands].

63 R&R, pp. 287–292.

The Cross now bears Christ's corpse. Though dead, at this moment he is King of the Jews and Lion of Judah: a matter on which Jennifer O'Reilly has written splendidly.[64] Lions were believed to sleep with their eyes open. While Christ's humanity sleeps in death, his invisible divinity, shared with the Father and Holy Spirit, watches over everything. In subjecting this innocent man to death, Satan has overreached himself: the gates of Hell are broken open so that the king of glory can come in. Adam and Eve and 'those who walked in darkness' are freed; a new creation has begun. The Cross now becomes protagonist, handing on Christ's wounded corpse to the care and contemplation of his followers. The narrative of this second *titulus* is based, not on the gospel accounts of how Jesus was taken down from the Cross and buried (Matthew 27:57–66 and parallels) but on the ways in which the Crucifixion was commemorated on Good Friday afternoon in the eighth century.

Directional symbolism gives the Tree panels and their *tituli* a cosmic dimension. We have moved from the inauspicious north side to the auspicious south. The Cross and Christ had both together endured mockery, but 'noble ones' now come 'eagerly' from afar, to Christ on the Cross (9). On the opposite side, the Cross had stood fast to raise the hero aloft (4). Now it, the surviving hero, bows to lay down and hand on his body. As the Cross 'beholds' the approaching nobles, it sings of its intense sorrow (11a), the only moment in the poem where sorrow is expressed. The 'noble ones' cooperate with the Cross, in sharp contrast to the mockers of the northern *titulus*. They lay down that 'limbweary' body, gather at its head and feet ('at the heads or both ends of his corpse') and 'behold' that corpse (14a) as the Cross had done (10b). The Cross displays not just sight but insight, compassion, grief, and concern for Christ's dead body: a much greater range of actions and human emotions than it did in the *titulus* on the north side. Here it becomes even more a model for 'noble' followers, on the first Good Friday and in later ages.[65] Between the two *tituli*, but especially in the second, the song of the Tree of Life gives a firm and comprehensive basis for devotion to the Cross.

This *titulus* is shaped to recall two scriptural passages: John

64 EMTI 1, Chapter 3, pp. 92–93, 98–100.

65 On early devotion to Christ's wounded body, see EMTI 1, Chapter 1, pp. 48–52; Chapter 5, pp. 143–146.

12:32, where Jesus had prophesied that 'if I be raised up from the earth, I will draw all things to myself' and Ephesians 2:13, 'now in Christ Jesus you who once were far off have been brought near by the blood of Christ'. Such passages had inspired the ceremonies commemorating the moment of Christ's death at the ninth hour (3 p.m.) on Good Friday. The roman ceremony, inspired by ceremonies at Jerusalem, was imitated and adapted to local needs throughout Europe. There was no Mass at Rome on Good Friday: the ancient 'meetings' ('synaxes') at the ninth hour preserved the practice of an early period when Mass was celebrated only on Sundays. Romans gathered in their various local churches. First, two Old Testament passages were intoned in the plainest of styles. The first, from the prophet Hosea (6:1–6), called for repentance, but promised 'on the third day [the Lord] will raise us up'. The second consisted of the Mosaic prescriptions for slaughtering the paschal lambs (Exodus 12:1–14), a good preparation for the Passion according to John, to follow. After the first reading the choir responded with an elaborate setting of 'Domine audivi' (Habbakuk 3). After the second reading the choir responded with an equally elaborate setting of 'Qui habitat' (Psalm 90/91). We will examine these chants later. Then, a cantor intoned, again in the plainest style, all of the Passion according to John (chapters 18–19). This uniquely presented the Crucifixion as taking place on 14 Nisan, at the hour when the paschal lambs were prepared for sacrifice. All those present, in due order, then kissed the relics of the Cross, which clerics presented to them before the altar. The Pope and his entourage came 'from afar', making a symbolic pilgrimage to Jerusalem. They walked barefoot from the 'basilica Salvatoris' (the Lateran, the Pope's cathedral), carrying the Lateran's relics of the True Cross, to the church called 'Hierusalem', some twenty minutes' walk towards the east. On their pilgrimage, they sang the great abcedarian Psalm 118/119 'Beati immaculati in via' ('happy are those on pilgrimage') important in Irish tradition as the 'biait'.[66] After each section of the psalm they chanted a refrain-like antiphon inviting bystanders to behold the cross-relics they carried ('Ecce'), and to join the procession ('venite'): 'Ecce lignum crucis, in quo salus mundi pependit: venite adoremus' ('Behold the tree of the Cross, on which hung the salvation of the world: come on, let us

66 HHBE, Chapter 9, pp. 237–8; R&R, p. 92 and n68.

adore'). At 'Hierusalem', when all had kissed the cross-reliquary, the Pope and his entourage returned directly with it to the Lateran, once more singing their pilgrimage-psalm or 'biait'. During the eighth century, an optional devotional extra was gradually introduced: people who asked could receive communion from loaves kept over in boxes from Mass on Holy Thursday, the day before. As people usually communicated under both species, bread and wine, they also had the more satisfactory option of attending other churches, where both were distributed. But the Pope and his court, following ancient custom, abstained from the Eucharist.[67]

Column IV (left-hand border)

12 [m]iþ s[t]rē[l]um ġiwundad
13 āleġdun hīæ hinæ limwœriġnæ ġistoddu[n] him [æt his līċ]æs [hea]f[du]m
14 [bih]ea[l]du[n] [h]ī[æ] þē[r] [heafunæs dryhtin] {…}

12 Wounded with arrows,
13 they laid him down, limb-weary. They stood at the head and feet of his corpse:
14 there they looked on [the Lord of Heaven] {…}

Jennifer O'Reilly's writing on early medieval devotion to Christ's wounded body enables us to understand the challenge this original narrative posed to the Ruthwell community.[68] Christ was 'limbweary': the four wounds in his limbs had brought him to the sleep of death (the spear-wound in his side was made after death). Had they, members of the Ruthwell community, themselves shot similar arrows at him? Arrows which wounded Christ must also have pierced the Cross: the *Dream* (62b) has the Cross say 'I was all wounded with arrows', clear evidence that some Anglo-Saxon audiences appreciated this idea.[69] St John's gospel had quoted the prophecy 'and again another passage of Scripture says, "They will look on the one whom they have pierced"' (19:34), a scriptural motif on which, as we have seen, Jennifer O'Reilly wrote eloquently.[70]

67 R&R, pp. 180–222.
68 EMTI 1, Chapter 1, pp. 48–54; Chapter 5, pp. 143–6; 2, Chapter 11, *passim*.
69 R&R, pp. 181–2.
70 See section 5, Moone.

Had members of the Ruthwell community ever sided with those who pierced him (and the Cross)? St Paul had claimed that 'I carry Christ's wounds [*stigmata*] on my body' (Galatians 6:17). Could they match Paul's claim? How could they participate in Christ's self-sacrifice?

12. The iconography of the second broad side

The second half of the cross (the second Tree of Life panel with its *titulus* which hints that we should follow our right hand *dessel*, sunwise, to the second broad side) is, like the first, structured as a gift-exchange between God and humankind. To understand this, we shall first examine the central panel of the broad side, and then the four panels that flank it in a double envelope pattern, above and below. This overarching pattern matches that spanning the first broad side. First, note a fascinating absence: this was the west side, and tradition held that Christ faced west on the Cross (see section 5): but there is no direct portrayal of the Crucifixion at Ruthwell, except the later addition on the other side of the base. Here, on the top border of the central panel, an alliterative acclamation in Latin proclaims that Jesus Christ is at once human and divine. As Jennifer O'Reilly showed, his personal name 'Iesus' was seen to refer particularly to his divinity, while the title 'Christ' referred primarily to his humanity.[71] In this acclamation, both natures are united. The context is one of judgement which, in the context of this second broad side of the cross, hints at the Parousia:

> Ieh*su*S XP*istu*S IVD[e]X AEQUVITATIS .
>
> Jesus Christ, the Judge of Fairness.

A rhythmical sentence on the panel's borders then calls him 'saviour of the world'. In the context of judgement, this title is hopeful:

> BESTIAE ET DRACON[ES] COGNOUERUNT IN DE/SERTO . SALVATOREM . MVNDI .
>
> Beasts and dragons recognised in the desert the Saviour of the world.

71 EMTI 1, Chapter 2, p. 83; Chapter 3, pp. 100–106; Chapter 6, pp. 169–186, 192–193; EMTI 2, Chapter 7, pp. 186–189.

Eagle and Rock
(mistakenly reversed from
first side: see p. 15)

Crosshead: Christ (in lost
central roundel) adored by
evangelists and their symbols

Matthew (right) and his
angel (left)

John the Baptist
acclaims Christ as Agnus Dei

upper stone

Two beasts acclaim Christ as
judge of fairness and saviour
of the world

Paul and Anthony recognise
Christ in sharing the loaf

Mary acclaims Jesus as a baby

Base: no sculpture,
originally buried

The verb 'cognoverunt' and the noun 'in deserto' are keys to the unity of the second broad side. This central panel primarily refers to Jesus' forty days' fast in the desert at the beginning of his public ministry, when 'he was with the beasts, and angels ministered to him' (Mark 1:13).[72] The penitential season of Lent was understood to be modelled on Christ's forty-day fast. Matthew's account (4:1–11) of Christ's triumph over the devil's temptations was intoned at Mass on its first Sunday. Commentators saw Christ's verbal victory over the devil to fulfil Psalm 90/91:13, 'you will tread on the asp and the basilisk, and tread down the lion and the dragon'.[73] Psalm 90 was central to the Mass chants of the first Sunday.[74] On Good Friday, all of Psalm 90 was sung again to an elaborate setting as the responsory to the second Old Testament reading (Exodus 12:1–14).[75] In response to the first reading (Hosea 6:1–6), an ancient setting of the Canticle of Habbakuk had already been sung. That long chant (the Old Latin translation of Habbakuk chapter 3) included the verse:

> In medio duorum animalium innotesceris,
> Dum adpropriaverint anni cognosceris,
> Dum advenerit tempus ostenderis in eo. (3:3)
>
> Between two living beings you will become known,
> When the years draw nigh you will be recognised,
> When the time comes you will be revealed.

The 'cognoverunt' of the *titulus* echoes the 'cognosceris' of the chant. The 'otterish' Ruthwell animals transform the usual iconography of Psalm 90:13. These anonymous beasts, crossing their paws between their bodies, have given up promising iconographic careers as lions and dragons, asps or basilisks to make Christ known in the desert 'in medio duorum animalium', 'between two living creatures'. Jennifer O'Reilly appreciated the joke that by their conversion the beasts and dragons of the desert may have been reshaped to recall the pair of sea-otters who between them warmed Cuthbert after his chilly sea-water vigil.[76] Their crossed paws, echoing the Greek

72 R&R, pp. 201–208.
73 EMTI 2, Chapter 7, pp. 183–186.
74 R&R, pp. 120–126.
75 R&R, pp. 184–187.
76 EMTI 2, Chapter 3, p. 59 (perhaps another Lindisfarne symptom?).

initial 'chi' ('X') of the panel's top border, proclaim 'Christ'. As the word 'krist' in the *incipit* of the second runic *titulus* has reminded us, they worship Christ's humanity, as Mary Magdalen does in tears at Christ's feet in the corresponding panel of the first broad side. To explain the transformed beasts, Jennifer O'Reilly was fond of quoting Bede's account of how Cedd's monastery had transformed Lastingham:

> Cedd chose himself a site for the monastery amid some steep and remote hills which seemed better fitted for the haunts of robbers and the dens of wild beasts than for human habitation; so that, as Isaiah says, 'In the habitations where once dragons lay, shall be grass with reeds and rushes', that is, the fruit of good works shall spring up where once beasts dwelt or where men lived after the manner of beasts.[77]

Above the beasts, Christ blesses with his right hand. He certainly blesses the scroll he holds in his left hand (the Book of Life?), but in view of the titles 'judge of fairness' and 'saviour of the world' it is reasonable to take it that his blessing includes the converted beasts and the onlookers. The 'bestiae et dracones' do not look downtrodden: rather they exult: like grateful Germanic warriors, they exalt their lord, the 'salvator mundi' who has transformed them. Their joy recalls the harmony between Adam and other living creatures in Paradise.

To understand how and why a Northumbrian designer should have transformed the standard iconography of Psalm 90:13, I now resort to a 'contrafactum' and write a sympathetic, not satiric, parody of how patristic writers thought in the words of scripture. In this I stay as close as I can to how orthodox writers interpreted scripture in eighth century Europe. They believed that Jesus, the Word of God, was in the beginning with God and was God (John 1:1). Together with the Father and the Holy Spirit, he had created the universe: without him was made nothing that was made (John 1:3); in him all things were created in heaven and on earth (Colossians 1:15). On the Friday morning of the first week of creation, God in Trinity had created birds and beasts. They created Adam in the image and likeness of God: patristic

77 Bede, *Historia Ecclesiastica* 3:23, quoting Isaiah 35:7; EMTI 2, Chapter 3, p. 60; HHBE, Introduction, p. xv.

commentators saw the Trinity as implied by the plural verb 'faciamus' in 'let us make man in our image and likeness' (Genesis 1:26). They placed Adam among the beasts in Paradise just before beginning the sabbath rest: say about the ninth hour on the first Friday (cf. Genesis 1:24–2:3). To reverse the damage done by Adam's fall, in the evening of the world Jesus himself chose to become human. He too became the image ('imago', Greek 'eikon') of the invisible God (Colossians 1:15), the second Adam (see section 6). He was humbler than the first Adam had been: as Gregory the Great put it 'he condescended to come, humble, to defeat the powers of the air' (quoted in section 11). For the joy that was set before him he heroically endured the cross and despised the shame that came with it (cf. Hebrews 12:2). That confidence was justified when, kenosis completed, the Father exalted him and gave him a name (Jesus) above every other name (Philippians 2:9–11: cf. section 11). Between two thieves on the Cross, his humanity and his divinity were both revealed.[78] God the Father willed that Jesus should hold 'primacy in all things'; in him all fullness should dwell (cf. Colossians 1:19–20). The designer therefore chose to place at the centre of this side an image in which Jesus appears as triumphant and kingly; kingly details are also to be seen in the 'Egypt' panel at the foot of this side. But the Father also willed 'through Jesus to reconcile all things to himself, making peace through the blood of his cross, both things on earth and things in heaven' (cf. Colossians 1:20). In heroic humility, the second Adam restored the harmony the first Adam had lost through pride. The mystery that restoration and reconciliation were achieved through the blood of the Cross was explored not only in the readings for the hour of Christ's death, but in the two solemn chants sung in response to the readings from the Tanakh. This was the only time in the liturgical year that these chants were sung together. They, and the lections they responded to, prepared for the intoned narrative of the Passion according to St John. The hour on which the devil was outwitted, and Paradise restored, involved forgiveness and compassion as well as the victory (Luke 23:34). To recall that hour, the Ruthwell designer transformed the traditional iconography of Psalm 90:13. Jesus, in the hour of his death, did not trample on any 'animalia', any of the living creatures he had himself created, not even those who pierced him

78 Bede, quoted at R&R, p. 207.

(John 19:34). Instead he reconciled them to himself and to the Father. In joyful gratitude, they acclaim him 'in medio duorum animalium', as in Habbakuk 3:3. The two joyful animals who acclaim him between their bodies stand for created creatures in general, and for the Ruthwell onlookers who acclaimed him as 'Jesus Christ the judge of fairness'. The Ruthwell designer placed at the centre of the west side of his or her cross an image of harmony restored in the *sacramentum* of Lent leading through the Crucifixion to Easter. Harmony restored implied Paradise regained. The designer's insight was imitated once, by the same school of sculptors, at Bewcastle; never again (as far as we know) in Northumbria, nor elsewhere in medieval Europe.

We have seen that many of the Irish crosses also contrasted Adam and Christ. They made the contrast by balancing images of Adam and Christ against each other on the base (see section 5, Moone), or above and below each other on the shaft (see section 6, Kells), or on opposite sides of the Cross (see section 8, Monasterboice). The Ruthwell designer not only transformed the iconography of the central panel to recall how the 'desert' trials of Lent were resolved in the Good Friday liturgy, he or she placed 'Christ acclaimed by the beasts' between two flanking panels which also refer to the ninth hour on Good Friday. At any time of the year all three panels would have recalled that solemn hour to nuns or monks of the Ruthwell community: the actions and atmosphere, the chants and intoned readings, and perhaps the procession 'to Hierusalem' singing the *biait* and its refrain 'Ecce lignum crucis'. A community who yearly participated in the *sacramentum* of Lent and Good Friday needed no further verbal explanation of the central panel, nor of the pair of panels that flanked and explained it.

If beasts and dragons can be transformed, so can communities. The central panel refers to the hour of Christ's death; the panels immediately above and below, forming an 'inner envelope' around 'Christ acclaimed by the beasts', symbolise the rites by which eighth-century communities participated in his death throughout the year. Breaking the loaf between their own bodies, Paul and Anthony also recognise Christ 'between two living creatures'. We have seen in section 2 that this panel may have been directly inspired by a courteous custom at Iona. The 'inner envelope' balances that reference to Iona with a reference to a new chant from Rome for the same moment of the Mass. On the upper stone, John the Baptist stands, as Paul and Anthony do in their panel. His gesture acclaims Christ as Lamb of God, an image central to the Good Friday readings (Exodus 12 and John 19). We have seen in section 9 that this panel 'grows out of' the Visitation on the opposite side, where the hidden John had acclaimed the hidden Messiah, and the *titulus* was 'hidden' in runes. In contrast, on this side both cousins appear in majesty, and are proclaimed in roman capitals. The fragmentary inscription, '[a]doramvs vt non cvm', 'We adore, so that not with', may possibly refer to I Corinthians 11:32, the earliest surviving account of a Eucharistic celebration (about AD 56), intoned in the Epistle for Mass on Holy Thursday (I Corinthians 11:20–32).[79] The word 'adoramus' seems to imply the Mass. To a mid-eighth century Northumbrian monastic audience the majestic image of John the Baptist would have recalled the new roman chant to accompany the breaking of the loaf, 'Agnus Dei, qui tollis peccata mundi, miserere nobis': 'Lamb of God, who takes away the sins of the world, have mercy on us'. The iconography of the panel is as innovative as the transformed 'beasts and dragons' in the panel just below, or the Paul and Anthony panel below that. It imagines John the Baptist as a figure within the heavenly liturgy.[80] He stands like the image of John the Baptist who is still 'standing in God's holy fire as in the gold mosaic' of the apse of the seventh-century chapel of San Venanzio at the Lateran baptistery. There his 'ancient' garments contrast with the well-trimmed 'contemporary' pallia and clerical garb of the two bishops to his left.[81] In the eighth century, a similar John the Baptist almost certainly stood (a replacement still stands), also right of centre, in the great golden apse mosaic of the Lateran basilica nearby. The apse of San Venanzio gives us an idea of what the image of the Baptist on that great apse may have looked like in the eighth century. That apse centred on a large bust portrait of Christ, a miraculous *acheiropita* (not made with human hands), placed just above an image of the glorified Cross on Calvary. From the hill (and from the Cross) flow the four rivers of a restored Paradise; between the rivers the heavenly Jerusalem can be seen.[82] The apse must have made a great impression on pilgrims; it, and the idea that

79 R&R, p. 183 and n12 on 214.

80 R&R, pp. 162–163.

81 R&R, pp. 234–236, figure 42(c) and plate 11.

82 R&R, pp. 233–234, figures 41 and 42(a).

the Cross was itself the sign of Christ, was important to Jennifer O'Reilly's teaching.[83] Earthly liturgies, transient and imperfect, were understood to be human efforts to copy the perfect liturgy of heaven: the gold mosaics of apses provided hints, during Mass and other liturgies, of what that heavenly liturgy might be like.[84] The heavenly and eschatological image at Ruthwell of John acclaiming Christ as Agnus Dei implies confidence that heaven approved the new 'Agnus Dei' chant, introduced into the Mass by Pope Sergius about AD 700.[85] It reminded any educated passers-by of the new chant, and perhaps encouraged them to sing to themselves *sotto voce* its confident prayer for freedom from and mercy for their sins. Though the chant had come from Rome, by the mid-eighth century it need not have been seen as exclusively 'roman'. It seems to have been known to Bede.[86] Caitríona Ó Dochartaigh has provided evidence to suggest that the new chant (as well as the 'Ave Maria' Offertory antiphon discussed above in section 9) may both also have been known to the Irish poet Blathmach, who wrote about AD 750–70. It is important to place that interesting possibility in the context of Jennifer O'Reilly's publications. She repeatedly challenged older assumptions, sad legacies of post-Reformation polemic, that Christians who followed 'celtic' and 'roman' traditions were usually in hostile rivalry to each other.[87] The 'inner envelope' on this broad side suggests that at Ruthwell the community welcomed ideas and chants from both traditions.

Both flanking panels refer symbolically, not literally, to the way the loaf was broken at Mass in both 'celtic' and in 'roman' rites. The actual rite, common to both traditions, took some time and involved the whole congregation. At the small monastic settlement of Derrynaflan, Co. Tipperary, the paten was about 36cm in diameter. The celebrant stayed silent, carefully cutting up the loaf on the paten. He first cut off a fragment from its right side and placed it in the filled and consecrated chalice, to symbolise the wounding of Christ's right side by the spear just after his death, the moment when

83 EMTI 2, pp. 57–58.

84 R&R, pp. 162–164, 232–233; EMTI 1, Chapter 5, pp. 143–146; EMTI 2, Chapter 7, pp. 170–179 and pp. 193–199; HHBE, Chapters 1 and 3.

85 R&R, pp. 247–259.

86 R&R, pp. 160–164, 247–257.

87 EMTI 1, Chapter 6; EMTI 2, Chapters 3 and 7; especially HHBE, Chapters 2, 3, 4 and 12.

blood and water flowed from his side, and Baptism and Eucharist were born.[88] He then broke or cut the rest of the loaf so as to provide a fragment for each communicant. Before distribution, he arranged the fragments carefully on the paten, sometimes in the shape of a cross. Each communicant knew that their fragment had just been cut or broken off from the communal loaf, Christ's body; their wine came from the communal chalice, Christ's blood. This protracted ritual must have been emotionally intense, as it symbolised the breaking of Christ's body by nails and spear on the Cross. In small community churches like Derrynaflan the communicants would have gathered round, standing close to the celebrant, experiencing how they and their community lived by sharing, via the Eucharistic loaf and chalice, in the body and blood of Christ.

When the new roman chant was sung, it was repeated as many times as was necessary to complete the ritual. While the chant went on, the priest in silence concentrated on cutting up the loaf and preparing the chalice for distribution. The gathered community sang the chant: other clerics, a choir if there was one, laity. It would have been easy to teach illiterate laity to join in for the final phrase 'miserere nobis' or a vernacular equivalent. The chant saw the Lamb as taking away the sins (plural) of all the world ('qui tollis peccata mundi') and asked for mercy for the community ('nobis', plural). This chanted plea for mercy recalls the emphasis on fairness at the top border of the 'beasts' panel, 'Iesus Christus iudex aequitatis'. The fragmentary *titulus* '[a]doramvs vt non cvm', on the lower border of this panel, runs parallel to that acclamation, and just above it.[89] Like the 'Agnus Dei' chant, both *tituli* combine acclamation and adoration with confidence in merciful judgement. Christians believed that when they broke the bread and drank the cup they 'showed forth the death of the Lord until he comes' (I Corinthians 11:26). The cross's programme, now coming towards its ending, turns to thoughts of last things and the return of Christ in glory at the second coming or Parousia. Jennifer O'Reilly wrote perceptively on this theme.[90]

The second, outer, envelope pattern spans and unites this side, from the 'Egypt' panel below to the crosshead above. At the foot

88 R&R, pp. 158–160.
89 R&R, p. 206, fig. 38(a)–(b).
90 EMTI 1, Chapters 1 and 6.

of the shaft a majestic Maria Regina acclaims her baby son. Jane Hawkes has demonstrated this panel to be an icon of 'Adventus': the little king advances, proclaimed by his queenly mother, to take possession of his kingdom. The Annunciation at the foot of the first broad side had inaugurated the images of growth on that side. Now Mary also inaugurates the central theme of the second broad side, acclamation and adoration of Jesus. Acclamation culminates in the quincunx of the crosshead, where a portrait of Christ in the lost central roundel (perhaps inspired by the miraculous Lateran *acheiropita* bust portrait?[91]) was acclaimed by the four evangelists. On the lower arm, Matthew still accompanies his angel; on the upper arm, John stands to contemplate his eagle. It is likely that on the missing transom Luke was paired with his ox and Mark with his lion, so that in the central roundel Christ was once more acclaimed between two 'animalia', ox and lion. As Matthew and John are also accompanied by living beings, the quincunx features four 'animalia': the central roundel was flanked vertically as well as horizontally (see section 3, the quincunxes symbolising Christ's wounds at Ahenny). During every Lent the *incipit* of each gospel was 'handed on', and its evangelist symbol explained, to catechumens and their families: the evangelist symbols were understood to be basic documents of the faith.[92] Jennifer O'Reilly has shown that the four symbols together were understood to provide a unified image of Christ, and a fourfold narrative summing up his kenotic expedition: 'born like a man, slaughtered like an ox, in Resurrection like a lion, in Ascension like an eagle'.[93]

On this second half of the cross, the Tree of Life once more sings in the persona of the Cross; it again provides the perspective needed to understand the broad side *dessel* or sunwise. The vernacular poem provides a moving image of how 'noble' followers should cooperate with the Cross in responding to the victory won when '[+] kris[t] wæs on rōdi' (see section 11). On this half of the cross, a vernacular chant in runic script once again leads sunwise to roman capitals and to *tituli* in Latin. Some of these, especially the acclamations, may well have been intoned, or set to more elaborate chants, by nuns or monks trained in local Northumbrian traditions of Old Roman chant.

91 R&R, pp. 34–35, figs 14 and 15.
92 R&R, pp. 143–146.
93 EMTI 1, Chapter 6, pp. 192–194.

That tradition had been renewed *viva voce* in the autumn and winter of 679 and the spring of 680 by John the Archcantor at St Peter's, Wearmouth when, as Bede tells us, 'all who were skilled in singing flocked in from almost all the monasteries in the kingdom to hear him, and he had many invitations to teach elsewhere'.[94] No doubt such oral traditions were often renewed and updated in later years by cantors accompanying such senior singers as Ceolfrid or Wilfred and Acca, or even clerics accompanying 'kings who opted out' such as Caedwalla of Wessex, baptised in Rome just before Easter 689 by Pope Sergius.[95] As Daniel Henry Haigh suggested in 1857, some of the Latin *tituli* may reflect locally-composed 'Latin antiphons, allusive to the subjects pourtrayed thereon, and those on its sides English verses descriptive of the Passion'.[96] The images and their Latin *tituli* point to the hope that the mystery of the Tree of Life and riddle of its runic *tituli* will finally be resolved, if only at the Parousia. The whole cross, in which vernacular chant and runic script consistently lead to Latin chant and roman capitals, celebrates that mystery.

The second half of the cross is structured as a sacred gift-exchange. Contemplation of Christ's wounded and exhausted corpse at the foot of the Cross on Good Friday evening leads to recognition and acclamation of him, communal sharing through the Eucharist in the life of the Trinity, and confidence that at the Parousia he will temper justice with mercy towards his sisters and brothers with whom he chose to become one flesh. The design of the Ruthwell Cross provides one intelligent Northumbrian reaction to Pope Sergius's recent Roman feast of the Exaltation of the Cross (14 September).[97] Sr Benedicta Ward correctly saw the Ruthwell Cross to be 'the first piece of systematic theology in Britain'.[98]

94 R&R, p. 224; see also pp. 92–93.

95 *Historia Ecclesiastica* 5:7; R&R, pp. 245–247, 261–266.

96 R&R, p. 26.

97 R&R, pp. 228–237; see the antiphon 'lignum vitae' in section 4 above.

98 *Journal of Theological Studies* 57 (2006), p. 279.

Printed in Great Britain
by Amazon

34607942R00036